I0177503

THE CASE

OF

THE MADIAI.

◆

POPISH PERSECUTORS

AND

FLORENTINE MARTYRS

In 1852.

BY

THE REV. W. P. LYON, B.A.

TUNBRIDGE WELLS:

STIDOLPH AND SONS, BATH SQUARE. NASH, LIBRARY.
NYE, GROSVENOR ROAD.

LONDON:

PARTRIDGE AND OAKEY, PATERNOSTER ROW.

Price Sixpence.

The following pages contain the substance of a Lecture delivered on the evening of the 25th November last, before "the Protestant Society for Tunbridge and neighbourhood." Of course, the lecturer alone is responsible for the publication. He has prepared these sheets for the press at the request of some who heard the lecture, and with the hope that they may aid in diffusing more widely a knowledge of the facts connected with this case of oppression, and of exhibiting the unrelenting and unchangeable character of the Romish Church as a persecutor. The detail of facts, as will be perceived, is taken chiefly from a work lately published under the title of "Prisoners of hope," to which the writer willingly acknowledges his obligations.

POPISH PERSECUTORS

AND

FLORENTINE MARTYRS,

In 1852.

———

FLORENCE is again acquiring an unenviable notoriety in the annals of persecution. In the year 1492, she startled Europe by the burning of Savonarola—a Dominican Monk, who, by his fearless and eloquent denunciation of the corruptions of Popery, seemed destined to effect the same work in Italy, which Luther afterwards accomplished in Germany. Now again, in the face of the advanced civilization and enlightenment of the latter half of the nineteenth century, similiar instruments of cruelty are there at work.—At Florence, not only is the Bible a proscribed book, but those who dare to read it, and follow out their convictions of its truth, are liable to fine and imprisonment; to solitary confinement and forced labour; to indefinite exile; nay, as appears from a decree issued on the 16th of this month, (Nov.) to death by the guillotine! Last year witnessed the banishment of Count Guicciardini, for being found with some friends in a private room reading the Scriptures. The present year will ever be memorable for the noble stand made for the rights of conscience and for Bible Christianity, by the Madiai, whose case is now exciting such sympathy and indignation throughout Europe. The following are the leading facts connected with this cruel and heartless persecution.—

About thirty years ago, a youth of 16, Francesco Madiai by name, came to Florence for medical aid, suffering under a complaint of the liver. His medical adviser, having succeeded in effecting a cure, ordered him to eat meat every day. He does so, and thus violates the well known law of the Romish Church, which forbids the eating of meat on Fridays. Being a sincere Romanist, his conscience is distressed by the commission of what he has been taught to regard as a sin, and Easter coming round, he goes to the cathedral to confess, and, as he hopes, to receive absolution. But how is he treated ? When the canon, to whom he makes his confession, hears that he has eaten meat, he turns on him in a rage, and shutting the door of the confessional in his face, says to him, ' thou art damned in body and soul.' Imagine the consternation of the youth at having such words addressed to him by one whom he has been taught to regard as standing almost in the place of God! The circumstance, however, tends to awaken his mind, and lead him to reflection.

Nineteen years pass away, and in 1840 we find him in Boston, in America. Some time previously to this he had become acquainted with the Scriptures. He finds nothing there about it being wrong to eat meat on Fridays, much less that he is liable to eternal condemnation on account of it. The conclusion he comes to is a very reasonable one. " The Priest has deceived me." The result is, he is convinced that Romanism is not in accordance with the Word of God. He therefore renounces it ; and in one of the Episcopal churches in Boston he receives the communion.

The narrative now carries us back again to Italy. He is a courier in the service of some English ladies. In their household he meets with Rosa, now his wife. They soon discover that their sentiments on religious subjects are similar ; and she, far in advance of himself, expounds to him, as Aquila and Priscilla did to Apollos, " the way of God more perfectly." Thus he advances in Christian knowledge. His faith is strengthened. He tastes the good word of God : and he who formerly had been threatened with eternal condemnation for eating meat on Fridays, now finds himself " justified by faith and having peace with God, through the Lord Jesus Christ."

In 1851 we find the Madiai settled in Florence. With a little money saved from their wages, they opened a boarding house in that city ; with the hope, from their being so well known to English families, that it would answer well. The circumstance which brought them under suspicion was the following. It appears that a servant who had lived with them for some time, and whose mind they hoped, had been enlightened by Divine truth, left their service, and went to reside with her mother-in-law The mother-in-law, a zealous Romanist, discovers that she possesses prohibited, that is, Protestant books, and makes this known *in the Confessional.* The girl is called up, and either through fear, or through bribery, most probably the latter, betrays all regarding the Madiai that she can betray. Now hear the result.—

On the 17th of August, last year, which was the Lord's day,—that day on which of all others we might have expected they would have been permitted to be in peace, —at $\frac{1}{2}$-past 7 o'clock in the evening, a party of gensdarmes visited their habitation. They were both from home, not being aware that any accusation had been lodged against them, or any suspicion regarding them entertained. The gensdarmes do not lose a moment. They search the house from the roof to the cellars. And what do they find ? Why, two copies of the Bible, some tracts, and a picture contrasting the errors of Popery with texts of Scripture. This is enough. Francesco, who comes home soon after, is at once arrested. Three individuals who have been waiting for him, one of them an Englishman, are also arrested, and their persons searched. Rosa, who has also come home, conducts herself with much calmness and propriety. She endeavours to cheer her husband—" You have done nothing wrong" she says to him, " You have done nothing to be ashamed of. Go without fear. Your innocence will be soon and easily proved, and in a few hours you will be liberated." Poor woman ! She did not know that it was a crime in Florence, to read the Word of God, and teach its sacred truths to others. She did not know that she herself had been guilty of crime in doing this, and that instead of her husband being soon liberated, as she hoped, she herself would soon be apprehended, to share with him a long and dreary, and cruel persecution, for her attachment to the Word of God!

On that Sunday evening, these four individuals were committed to prison. The Englishman was released after being detained for 22 hours. The other two, who were Florentines, confessed in their private examinations, that they read the Bible, and were Gospel Christians; and for this crime, and without any public trial, " they had the choice given them, either of indefinite imprisonment, or indefinite exile. Of course they chose the latter. And thus are these poor fellows, the one a shoemaker, the other a valet out of place, cast forth into the wide world as wanderers, without means, without friends, but such as Providence may raise up for them."

The Madiai were not so gently dealt with. For some reason or other—was it because English Christians who knew them, esteemed and respected them?—they were singled out as objects for special vengeance. Ten days after the arrest of her husband, Rosa, a feeble, sickly woman, suffering from a weakness of the spine, she too is arrested, and committed to the same close, filthy, unhealthy prison in which her husband is confined. But is she allowed to be with her husband? Is this little consolation permitted them in their affliction, of being locked up together? No! She has not been permitted to see her husband since that sad evening on which they were thus violently separated. She intreats it; pleads for it; but in vain. Her petition is harshly refused, and though in the same prison they are locked up in separate cells!

It was in the month of August, last year, when they were apprehended. From that time to December, nearly four months, they were not permitted to meet. *Then*, it seems, they had a brief interview *in the presence of their jailer.* Both had been suffering much from illness; yet they encouraged each other, and rejoiced together that they were counted worthy to suffer for the name of Jesus. After the lapse of about five months more, in the following April, they again had an interview, though only for a moment, and not with the consent of their persecutors. It appears that they were waiting one day in that month in separate but contiguous rooms, expecting to be called in for trial. The door between the rooms was opened, and they rushed into each other's arms. They were instantly and violently separated, and again locked up apart!

It was not till June last that they were brought to trial, so that they suffered a lingering confinement of about ten months, ere any attempt was made to prove them guilty of a crime. This was aggravated by repeated and distressing delays; the day of trial, after being fixed, having been again and again deferred. During this period, both suffered much in health, but their minds, were generally kept in great peace. On one occasion when some one remarked to Francesco that " perhaps the authorities were detaining him long in prison in order to induce him to recant, he answered warmly, ' I, abjure my faith and deny my Saviour! who even in my bonds, makes me so happy! never! they may do what they please with this poor body of mine, I may perhaps die in prison, but, with God's help, I will never deny Him; and what I say for myself, I am as sure of for my poor wife, who, weak and ill as she is in health, is firmer than myself in faith; well do I know this.'"

Much of his time was spent, while walking up and down his cell, in repeating psalms and portions of scripture, and in prayer: for by one of those refinements of cruelty in which the Romish Church is so skilled, they were not allowed to have the Scriptures, or any book of devotion they could use. Francesco passed six months in solitary confinement, before he was brought to trial.

"' It was the silence of the tomb. No sound of clock or bell reached him.' He asked, as a favour, to have his watch returned to him, as a companion; it was refused, and he patiently bore his disappointment. The window of his cell was built up, convent fashion, so as to admit light and air, but to exclude all view of the outer living world. Happy as he ever was, it was painful to see his physical, nervous derangement, in the twitchings of his face, and the trembling of his hands ; still was he more than conqueror through Christ strengthening him."

"Poor Rosa's Broken health, and highly nervous and sensitive temperament, caused her to feel her sufferings and trials more acutely, and sometimes she temporarily gave way to despondency and fear ; and deeply touching it was to witness her deep and humble contrition for her occasional lack of faith."

The defence of the Madiai was nobly undertaken by Maggiorani, a young man connected with the bar at Florence ; though, by so doing, he exposed himself to the hostile influence of the government. "Several who were asked, absolutely refused, saying, they had families, and they could not risk the ruin it might entail upon them."

The day of trial (June 5th,) at length arrived. On that day they were brought before the public tribunal, charged with the crime of "IMPIETY."

The following is the chief part of the act of accusation.—

As regards the Madiai, there has existed here for some time, and unhappily, it has been sought to propagate amongst us a heterodox confession called, "The Evangelical Religion, or Religion of the Pure Gospel," which, refusing, in many points, the Roman Catholic faith and discipline, and substituting private judgment concerning the knowledge and interpretation of the Scriptures, for the authority and traditions of the Church, impiously attempts to displace from the minds of the believers the pure and healthy principles of Catholicism, and to put in their stead false and condemned doctrines, to increase the number of its followers, and to enlarge its boundaries, to the insult and prejudice of our most holy religion, and the civil ordinances on which this rests.

To this confession belong Francesco and Rosa Madiai ; who, not content with having apostatized from Catholicism, in which they were born and brought up, have even sought to disseminate and insinuate into others their errors, without regard to age, sex, or condition, directing this wicked propaganda against the weakest and least experienced, placed, also, under their authority.

It is likewise ascertained that they lent their dwelling for the convenience of reunions, both for religious exercises and for the instruction of the members, particularly after these meetings were put down in other localities ; that such a reunion was held on the 17th of August last, when the public force discovered it, and made arrest, and perquisitions ; that at various times books, tracts, and heterodox works were deposited and kept there, and afterwards distributed by *decurioni;* that at the said reunion for instruction many came, even more than twenty Catholics (not excluding children,) some of whom thus imbibed and were confirmed in the errors of their sect; and that the Madiai, even out of this reunion profited by every favourable occasion to exercise proselytism, preaching and insinuating, amongst other things, maxims contrary to the sacrament of Confession, to the real presence in the Holy Eucharist, to the sacrifice of the Mass, to the doctrine of Purgatory, to the worship of the Sacred Image, to the intercession of the Blessed Virgin and the Saints, to the Priesthood, to the Pontificate, to the observance of certain Feast days, to the forbidding of certain food, &c. They also distributed Bibles translated, and not approved by the Church, and books of prayers corresponding with the errors mentioned.

Some persons declare that they refused to join in spite of repeated insistance; others that they incurred the risk of falling; and one (Antonietta Marsini, their servant) confessed that she indeed fell into error, so far as to partake twice of the Communion that they celebrate in commemoration of the Last Supper, and to follow in some things Rosa Madiai, who urged her to break the beads of her rosary and the scapulary she had on her neck, as being objects of idolatry.

The Madiai confess to their apostasy, and deny the proselytizing, but admit having taught the truth to those who sought it from them. They are contradicted in this by not a few witnesses.

In consequence, Francesco, son of the late Vincenzio Madiai, 48 years old, married, without children, native of Diaceto, in the prefecture of Pontassieve, living in Florence, a courier, and letter of lodgings; and

Rosa, daughter of the late Stefano Pulini, wife of the said Madiai, native of Rome, living in Florence, aged 50;

Are accused of impiety.   *   *   *   *   *   *   *   *

Written at the office of the Royal Procurator General, at the Royal Court of Florence, 6th December, 1851.

A. BICCHIERAI, Royal Proc. Gen.

It will be observed that the crime with which the Madiai are charged, springs entirely from their religious profession. No charge is brought or can be brought against their moral character. They are admitted in this respect to be *irreproachable.* The public prosecutor, in his speech on the trial, says, " The acts of goodness, natural probity, and benevolence, that Madame Madiai wished to urge in arrest of judgment, may cause one to grieve more over her separation from Catholicism, but cannot free her from the present crime, and

accusation, nor diminish the imputation cast upon her."
Nor can any charge of political conspiracy be brought
against them. The public prosecutor distinctly admits
this, affirms it, reiterates it. He says, " of direct political elements, the cause of the Madiai offers no trace.
They figure in it solely for the religious element, and for
the consequences this produced upon public order . . .
We cannot affirm, nor do we allege that the Madiai
knowingly worked as the instruments or organs of any
political sect."

It is thus admitted by the public prosecutor himself,
that the Madiai are suffering purely for conscience sake.
They are charged with "impiety," but their impiety
consists in having left the Romish Church, and embraced
the confession of the pure Gospel; and in their venturing
to possess and study the sacred Scriptures, and instruct
any who came to them for the purpose, in Scripture
truth. The following is an account of the trial.—

On the morning of the 5th of June, the long expected trial of
Madiai and his wife commenced ; they were placed in the dock
guarded by several gensdarmes; they looked calm and dignified,
and quietly awaited the entrance of the lawyers, and bench of six
judges, who also acted as jury. Francesco appeared so pleased at
once more seeing his wife, and pressed her hand. The attorney
general opened the case, and proposed that the trial should be private ; this being agreed to by the judges, the court was cleared of
all the reporters, and most of the Italians ; several English, and
some of the Italian Christians, were allowed to remain, about eighty
or hundred having, like myself, obtained permission from one of the
secretaries to stay ; there were also a great many priests present.
Witnesses for the prosecution were next examined by the judges,
and in a way that clearly showed the sentence on the Madiai had already been determined on. Words were often put into witnesses'
mouths, when they seemed at a loss, and they professed to remember nothing when their evidence was contrary to the written statement which had been taken down from their lips, on previous examinations. I could not but be astonished at the barefaced shame-
lessness with which the bench thus carried on the prosecutions.

In the course of this examination, Count Guicciardini's confession
of faith was read out, and many tracts which had been found in
the Madiai's rooms were also read out in full, and a picture also
found there, which represented the errors of Popery contrasted with

texts of Scripture, was produced, and the texts, &c., which were in English, translated into Italian; thus much truth reached the ears of the judges and audience. Francesco also frequently quoted Scripture when he was asked about his religious opinions; this made the judges very angry, and the president frequently forbade him to quote the Bible, as they did not wish to hear his religious dogmas. Nothing could exceed the Christian behaviour of both Francesco and Rosa. *She* was particularly sustained, and all who heard her frequently exclaimed in a whisper, with how much dignity and propriety she gave her answers, especially when one of the judges wished to confuse her by a series of irrelevant cross questions; several times she silenced him by her replies, amidst evident sensation throughout the court; and once he threw himself back in his chair in complete confusion, when she was declaring in what her change of religion consisted. Madiai, also, in questioning some of the witnesses, spoke to them in a very Christian and even tender way, lamenting their unfaithfulness, and the falsehood they uttered. To one he said, "Go! my chains are of much greater value than all the false evidence which thou hast given against me." Upon which the president of the court in a rage told him "Not to make a martyr of himself, and not to utter one word more than was necessary, especially before a Catholic public."

The examination against them lasted two days, and some clever legal men declared that there was not *one word* or incident which in any way rendered them guilty—supposing even all that had been said against them was true. They proved that the Madiai had ever respected the opinions of others, and had by no means attempted to proselyte to their own opinions, *in the manner that their accusers contended*—for conversion, they said, can only be from God. Their testimony brought to light most beautiful traits of Christian love and conduct in the accused, and nothing appeared which could in any way dim the integrity of their private life. In the course of the defence Madiai was asked "if he was not born in the bosom of our holy mother the Roman Catholic Church?" he answered, "Yes, but I am now an Evangelical Christian." "Who made you such, and does any act of abjuration exist in the hands of those with whom you have united yourself?" "My convictions have existed for many years already, they have acquired strength through the study of the Word of God; it is a thing entirely between myself and God, which nevertheless was openly manifested when I took the communion in the Swiss Church." Rosa replied to her interrogator that "she had not lightly changed her religion, or to please man, since in that case she would have done it in England, where she had lived for sixteen years; but that after having read much and studied the Word of God, and compared it with the doctrines of the Roman Church, she had remained convinced, and had abandoned that Church, and that she had chosen the moment to make her public confession of faith, by taking the communion, when the laws gave and protected the liberty of citizens." (This must have been in 1848.)

There were twelve witnesses against, and six for, the Madiai; and, finally, Maggiorani, the counsel for the prisoners, closed the case, by making a speech which lasted three hours, setting forth first the legal question, and closing with an analysis of the evidence against them, and completely showing how false it all really was. The attorney-general replied, and ended by advising the judges to sentence the prisoners, Francesco to fifty-six months' solitary confinement and hard labour, and Rosa to the same, for a period of forty-six months. The court was then closed, and all went away; notice was given that sentence would be pronounced on the following day.

The Bench deliberated that same evening for three hours, without being able to come to any conclusion. The next day at ten o'clock, the whole place was filled with persons of all classes; the Bench had already been deliberating since nine o'clock, but half-past two came, and still they could not agree, and we began to hope for a favourable sentence; at length, at half-past three, after nine and a half hours' deliberation, the judges entered the court. It now appeared that the cause of their long deliberation was, that they could not agree; some desiring a milder sentence, and the president himself at length gave the casting vote for the condemnation of the accused. The sentence was (to the astonishment of all) exactly that which had been asked for by the attorney-general. The ten months which they had already passed in prison were not to be reckoned as part of the sentence. Besides this, they are to be subjected to three years' surveillance of the police after the term of their imprisonment is ended. (The surveillance of the police is most harassing; they enter your house as often as they please during the day, or in the dead of night. You must show yourself to them whether you are sick or well, and must never be out of your house after eight o'clock in the evening, &c.) All the expenses of the trial are also to be paid by the Madiai.

At the close of the sentence, both immediately arose from off their seats, and looked at each other, as if greeting one another after many months' absence, they then shook hands, both smiled on each other, embraced, and in a few moments disappeared amidst the bayonets of their guards.*

In these extracts, it is stated to be the opinion of able legal men, that "even supposing all that was said against the Madiai to be true," they were not guilty of any violation of the law under which they are now suffering. Here is that law.—

"Whosoever, with an impious intent, shall dare to "profane the divine mysteries, by disturbing the sacred "functions with *violence,* or shall otherwise commit any

* " Prisoners of Hope." p p. 62-8.

"*public* impiety, and who shall teach *publicly* maxims
" contrary to our Holy Catholic religion, towards which
" we have always nourished, and will perpetually nourish,
" our constant love and zeal, we will that he, as a dis-
" turber of the order by which society itself is ruled and
" maintained in tranquillity, shall be punished with the
" greatest and most exemplary rigour, never with less
" punishment than public labour, for a time or for life,
" according to the circumstances of the case."†

But this law, unjustifiable and iniquitous tho' it be,
was not violated by the Madiai. It embraces three classes of offences, to any one of which *publicity* is essential.
The first is " disturbing the sacred functions with violence." It is not pretended that they have been guilty
of this. The second is " committing any *public* impiety."
Nothing of this kind is charged against them. The third
is " teaching *publicly* maxims contrary to the Catholic
religion." Have they been guilty of this? No, verily!
They had too much of the spirit of humility to set themselves up as *public* teachers. They only taught *privately*
those who applied to them for instruction. But then it
has become " public and notorious" that they have done
so; and hence argues the prosecutor, " publicity in the
sense, and for the requirements of the law is not wanting! We shall give this passage as it stands in his
published speech.——

"For the rest, it was public and notorious that there
existed a Confession of the Pure Gospel; public and
notorious that this was directed against Catholicism, and
loudly and unweariedly declared against certain legisla-
tive and government measures; public and notorious
that the Madiai belonged to the same Confession; finally,
public and notorious (and this is to the point) that they
took part efficaciously and heartly in the propagation of
the false doctrine, in the distribution of wicked books; so
that the priest of their parish felt himself compelled to
make a report of it to the episcopal authority, to be en-
abled to provide a remedy, as it treated really of doctrine,

† " Trans. Act of Accusation," J. C. Evans, Esq.

Thus, publicity in the sense and for the requirements of the law was not wanting; on the contrary, it was great, therefore scandalous and highly hurtful."*

Admirable specimen of jesuitical reasoning! Worthy of a disciple of that master who requires his followers to pledge themselves to be ready, if needful, for the good of the church and " the greater glory of God," to swear that black is white, and that white is black! A thing done in *private* becomes a thing done in *public*, when it is known and notorious that it has been done in private! That is to say, what is white becomes black, when it is known and notorious that it is white! But in the Romish Church, the end sanctifies the means! Wrong becomes right, and the most abominable injustice is perfect righteousness, when perpetrated to put down heresy!

An appeal was made to the Supreme Court against the sentence passed on the Madiai, but without effect. A petition on their behalf, was then presented to the Grand Duke, the reigning sovereign of the country. It was peremptorily rejected. The following is an account of the way in which the sufferers received the intimation.—

The petition for grace was peremptorily rejected! This summary proceeding, which allowed no opportunity for the interference of the Prussian or English Minister, was known to a few on Monday. Maggiorani (their lawyer) was absent at Leghorn, and did not hear of it till Tuesday, when he immediately returned here. We went together to the Murate prison; Madiai was in perfect peace, he received the final blow in a spirit of holy submission, and the only expression of suffering was, squeezing my hand, saying, "there is need of patience," but cheerfulness beamed in his countenance, although suffering from continual physical illness; he also said, "The comfort and joy of the Holy Spirit never changes with me; however it may be with my poor body, I am always happy; God has been with me all the time of my imprisonment, and He will always be with me as long as I remain in prison, and I am as sure that He will be with me unto death." He wished to have with him a supply of clean linen, &c., adding, " if permitted;" we found on inquiry, that *this was not permitted;* he instantly smiled, saying, "Well, all things according to the will of God." He talked beautifully about his wife; and requested me to tell her, that his prayer was that God would go with them to their prisons, and that he felt sure that God would be their companion there.

* " Prisoners of Hope," p. 115.

Afterwards we went to the Bargello: her sufferings were great, but they speedily assumed the character of Christian fortitude. She at once took leave of the various topics of hopes and fears which had long kept her noble spirit in painful exercise, and turned at once to her strong-hold. "Tell all," she said "not to pray for our liberation, but for that increase of faith which may enable us to suffer cheerfully." And then before us all and the attendants, she burst forth into fervent prayer, especially for more faith, more love to Jesus! The doctor was in the prison at the time; she sent for him; I was much pleased with him, and although it was unusual, he said he could give her a certificate as to the state of her health, requiring diet different from that of the common prisoners, as absolutely important for her life. We remained an hour with her. Maggiorani has fixed to go to Lucca to see that everything is provided that can be permitted, and perhaps I may go also.

This morning early, I received a most unexpected notice from one of the prison officers, that she was going off instantly, and wished to see me. I filled a small basket with tea, sugar, &c. When I arrived at the Bargello, K—— very kindly let me go to her cell. I found her meeting this trying moment most nobly. She explained to me, that she wanted her bonnet, gown, shawl, &c.; these were under the care of W——. I soon brought them. She asked me to leave her for a few moments, when she quickly dressed and appeared smiling. She said, "I have done nothing to my hair, for they will cut that off." She sent much love to you all, and so did he, mentioning you by name; she said with much feeling, "Remember me to all the brethren, and tell them, should they be called to follow us, to bear what may be appointed them to suffer, but never to forsake their God! I desire not only to take up the Cross, but to bear it cheerfully with abounding thanksgiving. What an honour it is for such unworthy creatures to be called to suffer in the Lord's cause." I handed her into the carriage, and we parted under a great blessing. She was attended by a female jailer and some gensdarmes. I can give you no account of his departure to Volterra; no doubt he is gone. What barbarity, thus to separate husband and wife, who have never met since their trial.*

Nor have they met to the present hour! The following letter, written by Rosa to her husband after the trial, presents a fine specimen of Christian heroism.

MY DEAR MADIAI,—Thou knowest how I have always loved thee; how much more, then, must I love thee now, that we have been together in the battle of the Great King, and that tho' cast down, we have not been vanquished. I hope that through the merits of Jesus, God the Father has accepted our testimony, and that He will give us grace to drink, even to the last drop, the bitter

* "Prisoners of Hope." p.p. 80-3.

cup which is prepared for us, and that, too, with thanksgiving. My good Madiai; our life—what is it? A day, a day of grief; yesterday, young; to-day, old; but, nevertheless, we can say with old Simeon—"Now lettest thou thy servant depart in peace, since *our* eyes have seen thy salvation." Courage, my beloved; since we know, by the Holy Ghost, that *that* Christ who was laden with reproach, trodden under foot, and despised, is our Saviour, and we, by the effect of his light and power, have taken upon us the defence of the cross, bearing his reproach, so that one day we may share his holiness and glory. Do not fear, if our condemnation be severe; God, who caused the chains to fall from Peter and opened the gate of his prison, will not forget even us. Be of good courage; let us cast ourselves entirely into the hands of God; let me see thee joyful, as I hope, through the same grace, thou wilt see me joyful.

With all her heart embraces thee,
Thy affectionate wife,

June 7th, 1852.§ Rosa Madiai.

The case of these sufferers for the truth's sake, as soon as it became known, excited among Protestants of all denominations, a great amount of sympathy. When the fact of their condemnation, and the failure of the attempts that had been made to procure the cancelling of their sentence, became public; meetings for prayer on their behalf, and also for the expression of the indignant feeling of the Christian public at their cruel persecution, were held at numerous places in this country and on the continent. The Protestant Alliance nobly bestirred itself for their deliverance; and on the suggestion of Sir Culling Eardley, it was resolved that a deputation should visit Florence to seek an interview with the Grand Duke, and endeavour to procure their release. It soon appeared that Continental Christians also wished to share in the good work. It was determined, therefore, that the deputation should have a European character; and while the British Churches were represented in it by two of our Nobility—the Earl of Roden, and the Earl of Cavan, along with Captain Trotter; it included in it deputies from the Christians of France, Switzerland, Holland and Germany.

The formation of this deputation affords one of the finest manifestations of Christian union which can

§ " Prisoners of Hope." p.p. 71-2,

be found, perhaps, in the entire history of the Church. It has long been the boast of Rome that she possesses *unity.* Romanists point to the separation of Protestants into different denominations as a proof that they have no unity : and if unity (they argue) be a mark of the true Church, then must Protestants be wrong, because they are divided, and Romanists be right, because they are one. It would be easy to show that this unity of the Romish Church is a pure fiction, and that, boasted of everywhere, it is to be found nowhere ! Take, for example, their differences of opinion on one of the fundamental points—viz. infallibility. They say that their church is infallible ; but if we ask them where this infallibility lies, how many different replies do we receive ! Some say "in the Pope, the Head of the Church." Others say " nay, the infallibility is with the body of Pastors, joined with their head." Others reply, "not so, the infallibility resides in the councils of the church." And others, again, remonstrate against this idea, and plead that it is in the *entire* church ; in the unanimous consent of all her members, in all places and at all times. Here then is one specimen of Romish unity. They everywhere agree that their church is infallible ; they everywhere disagree as to where this infallibility is lodged. " To be sure," they say " we have it, tho' we don't know where ! We are agreed that it is *some where* in our church, tho' we are not agreed as to where that some where is ! "

Protestant Christians possess a better—a truer unity than this. They have " the unity of the Spirit"—the unity which results from that Spirit which dwells in Christ, dwelling also in all the members of which his church is composed. If there be *minor* points of belief on which they differ, on the great essentials of Christianity they are entirely agreed. If they are not quite of one mind, they are at least of one heart. Behold a proof of it ! Here are two individuals of humble birth, and occupying but a humble position in life, cruelly persecuted because of their attachment to the Word of God, and their determination to follow out their convictions of its truth. This becomes known. The tidings of it spread rapidly from one end of Europe to the other. A deep feeling of sympathy for them is at once awakened among Christians of all denominations. Numerous meetings are held to express their sympathy, and to offer prayer for them ; and English and Continental noblemen and gentlemen willingly undertake a mission to the far away place of their captivity, that they may pour the balm of consolation into their wounded spirits, and adopt all those measures which Christianity will sanction, to mitigate their sufferings, and procure their release. These gentlemen go, armed with no weapon but " the Sword of the Spirit, which is the word of God." They willingly avow that their own faith is the same as that of the persecuted sufferers ; that they regard them as one with themselves in Christ ; and love and honour them all the more that they are thus encountering shame and imprisonment, the loss of property, and exposure to death for His name's sake. We are here reminded of another sufferer, who was once languishing in prison for the same cause, in another city of that Italian Peninsula, and of his grateful remembrance of a Christian friend, who sought him out in the place of his confinement, that he might cheer him by his sympathy, and minister to his relief. *" The Lord,"* says he, *" give mercy unto the house of Onesiphorus; for he oft refreshed me, and was not ashamed of my chain : But, when he was in Rome, he sought me out very diligently, and found me. The Lord grant unto him that he may find mercy of the Lord in that day."* 2 TIM. 1. 16-18.

The members of this deputation may be congratulated that they followed in the footsteps of one whom this first of the Apostles remembered with such grateful interest and affection.

It was not to be expected that this deputation should be successful. If the remonstrances of the King of Prussia, and (we are happy it can be added) the remonstrances of Royalty in our own country, failed to procure their release : it was not to be hoped for that those of the deputation would be effectual. The following is their published report.

"In reporting upon the results of our mission, we have to state that, in accordance with what we understood to be the views of those whom we represent, we, in our first communication with the Tuscan Minister for Foreign Affairs, disclaimed the advancement of any political object, or the use of any political assistants; aiming to approach the Grand-Duke in the character solely of Protestant Christians, who sympathized with the position, and desired to alleviate the actual condition of our imprisoned brother and sister, Francesco and Rosa Madiai. We would further state, that in order to attain our object of an audience with the Grand-Duke, we scrupulously avoided putting forward our firm conviction of the injustice and cruelty of the sentence under which they are confined. Our task was not to demand what we believed to be justice, but to ask that which would be deemed by the Grand-Duke the exercise of mercy.

" Notwithstanding the conciliatory spirit in which our request for an audience was conceived, and the grounds thereof stated, we regret to have to announce that our application was refused. As it is our wish to narrate everything with moderation, we would add that this refusal was couched in courteous terms As regards the great object of our mission, it is but too evident that the hope held out of mercy is most vague; nevertheless, as the language used would seem to justify a hope, we cannot but trust that it may be speedily realised.

" With the termination of our mission, we consider it our duty to acquaint those whom we represent, and the Christian public generally, with the actual position of the Madiai. Not having as yet had the privilege and advantage of personal access to them, we proceed, from information on which we can fully rely, to present their condition accurately; avoiding everything in the way of exaggeration, not only for the sake of truth, but because it is a melancholy fact that sufficient of grevious hardship exists to excite the warm indignation, and enlist the active sympathies, of Protestant Christendom.

"The Madiai, then, are not sentenced to the galleys, nor are they confined in chains, nor placed in the same cells with felons. They are treated with kindness by the attendants in the prison; but their sentence has been not only for a term of imprisonment of unusually long duration, but one which has attached an unjustifiable stigma of infamy to them. Their confinement is solitary, and involves with it labour *(travaux forces.)* Considering the activity of Francesco Madiai's past life as a travelling courier, and the extreme delicacy of his wife Rosa from spinal disease, it is no matter of surprise that this confinement should have proved most injurious to the health of both; and fears are to be entertained as to a fatal issue, if it be much further prolonged. What would be the sensation in Europe, if any such sad termination to their present sufferings should ensue? We ought here to notice their total deprivation of all public worship, and the consolation of a minister of their own faith—privileges which would be most precious to them, and which are amply afforded to every other, even the very worst offenders, confined within the same prisons. They are separated from each other, not only in different cells, but in different prisons; the one on the heights of Volterra, the other fifty miles off, in Lucca; as if the intercourse of these poor sufferers could be dangerous to the State; so that to the hardships already alluded to is added an agonising uncertainty as to the health of each. They are denied the use of such devotional or other books as may be in accordance with their own views. When allowed to take exercise, they are obliged to do so in a confined space, between high walls, which shut out the view of everything except the sky.

"Lastly, with respect to the trial and sentence. Although the evidence was not allowed to be published *in extenso,* we may state, on the authority of those who were present at the trial, that it was distinctly proved that the life of Rosa Madiai had been for years marked by acts of charity and love, without reference to the peculiar faith of those whom she succoured; that upon these occasions she made no use of such opportunities to assail the religious principles of those whom she benefited. The few acts of controversial discussion deposed to against them were in answer to, or in consequence of, the applications or arguments of those who themselves entered into discussion with them. It resulted from the whole trial, that publicity—an essential element of their crime under the law by which they were tried—was so completely and, on the face of the sentence, so confessedly wanting, that the bench (who acted both as judge and jury) were obliged to base their conviction upon the general course of jurisprudence as exhibited in former decisions. These decisions were, however, shown to be inapplicable, or, even, if applicable, not sufficient to warrant any such severity of sentence. It is further worthy of notice, that this incongruity between the law under which they were tried, the case under which they were convicted, and the sentence under which they are suffering, was, independent of the facts, made the ground of formal appeal on the part of their counsel, Signor Maggiorani, whose name deserves to be noticed by us with gratitude, not more for the talent and legal knowledge which he displayed, than for the boldness of his professional conduct, and the tender and considerate assistance which he has privately afforded to his oppressed clients. It should be added, that the arguments of Signor Maggiorani on this point were formally and publicly assented to as sound and valid, under the signature of others most eminent at the Florentine bar. An appeal for further argument in the case was not only not opposed, but was advocated by the counsel for the Crown; and yet such appeal was ineffectual.

"We have preferred a temperate and accurate statement of facts to any, the most eloquent, appeal to your feelings. What our feelings are may be easily conceived; suffice it to say, that they impel us to urge a loud and continued protest against a sentence of imprisonment thus inflicted; involving with it bodily suffering, and even risk of life, together with religious privations from which all offenders in every civilised country are exempt.

"The report, which we have thus laid before you, would not be complete were we to leave the impression that this is but a solitary instance of suffering for Christ's sake. The case of the Madiai is but the type of a numerous class; for it is an awful fact that the progress of persecution is fearfully advancing. It would, therefore, be desirable that the publicity which its peculiar circumstances have obtained for it should attract attention to very many others, in order to make them the subject of our earnest prayers and efforts. We do not exaggerate when (in the very terms of the persecution of the first Christians) we affirm that a system prevails here of " entering into every house" where suspicion, not of political but of religious " crime" exists, " haling men and women, committing them to prison," and " breathing out threatenings." We might tell, with truth, of not a few " put into the common prison," of several " scattered abroad," and of very many who, hungering and thirsting after these privileges, are prevented meeting for prayer and the study of the Bible. We can only say, in conclusion, " My brethren, ' these things ought not so to be.'" How they are to be remedied may be considered by others possessing more worldly wisdom than ourselves. In the meantime, we cherish the hope that, when and how the Lord may see fit, He will vindicate His own cause, and deliver those who are persecuted for His name's sake."

RODEN, CAVAN, JOHN TROTTER, British Deputation. HENRY TRONCHIN, ALEX. H. DE ST. GEORGE, Swiss Deputation. GRAF ALBERT VON POURTALIS, A VON BONIN, German Deputation. F. DE MIMONT, French Deputation. ELOUT DE SOCTERWONDE, Deputation for Holland.

We do not wonder that the Grand Duke refused to meet these gentlemen. We hope for the sake of humanity, it was a feeling of shame that prevented him. It appears that subsequently to this report being written, Lord Roden was permitted to visit in their prisons, these sufferers for the Gospel's sake. " I visited," he says, " the Ergastolo prison, at Lucca, at one o'clock on the 31st of October, and was met at the door by the direttore (governor.) . . . I told him that I had some letters for Rosa, and begged to know if I might give them to her. He said it was his duty to read her letters first, so I gave them to him. We soon reached the door of the cell in which she was confined; when opened, there was presented to my view a rather tall figure, with a very interesting countenance, apparently about fifty years of age, dressed in the striped habit of the prison, with a cap on her head of the same materials, her hands and face delicate and pale. Notwithstanding her prison clothes, she appeared, in her manners and address, far superior to the station which she had filled in society. The direttore asked her if she knew who I was? She said not; not being aware that any one was coming to visit her. He told her that I was Lord Roden. She then pressed my hand, saying, How could she ever thank me enough; that she knew she could never give any return to her *bienfaiteurs* but her prayers. I told her I had come to-day with the expression of the deepest sympathies of Christian men, from England, France, Germany, Switzerland, and Holland, to convey to her their feelings for her and her husband, which had led them to leave their homes as humble suppliants to the Grand Duke on their behalf; that he had refused to see us; but that, in his reply to our application, he had spoken of the time and moment of grace being in his own power; by which we hoped that he had in view a time for the exercise of mercy towards them, and that we trusted and believed that it would not be long delayed. I reminded her that she was suffering for Christ's sake, and that she was not the first who had suffered. She then immediately referred to the case of Joseph, who, though innocent, had been put in prison like her. I remarked, " Yet see how God turned it to Joseph's benefit, and to His own glory;" that Peter and Paul, and others, had been also honoured as she was honoured; and that we, who had come to Tuscany to assist her and her husband, if in our power, while partakers with them by deep sympathy in their sufferings, participated also with them in their honour; for it was written, " Whether one member suffer, all the members suffer with it; or one member be honoured, all the members rejoice with it." (1 Corinth. xii. 26.) She then spoke of the conduct of those who had falsely sworn against her, to whom she had been so kind a friend. "Well," I said, "do not think of them, except to pray for them." She said she did this. I added, "Remember what charges were brought against our Lord and Master, and how he prayed, even for His murderers." I asked whether the Lord Jesus was her strength and comfort?" to which she replied, "Oh, how could I have gone through what I have, now a prisoner for fifteen months, if it had not been for him!" I enquired if she had any religious books? She pointed to a few by her side, among which was a Roman Catholic Bible.

" I then interrogated her about her food. She said she had now bouillon every day, and meat twice a week; and on other days two eggs; and though she did not wish to complain, she could not but feel the contrast between this diet and her former comfortable mode of living. . . . I was much struck with Rosa's forbearance, in not alluding to the unwholesome diet and barbarous treatment, to which she was subjected in the *Bargello,* the common prison of Florence, for many months previous to **her** being committed to the *Ergastolo.* I thought it would be useful to tell her before the direttore and the matron, who were present during the whole of my visit, of the great interest which her case had excited in Europe, in order to draw forth a continuation of their kindness to her. I made known to her the anxiety which the King of Prussia had shown, by sending Count Arnheim, a Prussian nobleman, specially from Berlin, to plead her cause before the Grand Duke. She said she understood that he, having heard at Genoa of his refusal to see us, had not come on to Florence, as also the deputies who were on their way thither. I told her she was quite mistaken, as they were all now at Florence, and that my brother deputies had sent in their petition to the Grand Duke for an audience, but had been also refused. . . . When I saw that the direttore had read the letters which I had put into his hand, I asked him whether she might have them. He said, "Yes," and put them on the table. I never saw a more melancholy object, nor such an instance of the effects of bigotry, tyranny, and cruelty—this dear servant of Christ, a woman of superior mind, education, and appearance, bent down to the very lowest state of depression, by an incarceration of fifteen months, for reading and openly confessing the Word of God! I told her that I hoped to see her husband the day after to-morrow, and asked her if she had any message for him? She said none; except to tell him that she was well. I replied, "How can I tell him that, as you look so poor and delicate?" "O, I am well," was her answer, "in comparison to what I was; but I suffer from a spinal complaint which afflicts me greatly sometimes; I wrote to him yesterday." . . .

"There were many other interesting details in our conversation, which, for brevity's sake, I omit. I parted from her with a prayer, that God might look upon her still in His great compassion, and support and strengthen her to the end. Much affected, she pressed my hand, and I turned my back on a scene which I can never forget. I heard the heavy bolt of the cell door, which again closed on this "prisoner of Jesus Christ" (Philemon 1,) suffering for His name's sake, and I retraced my steps to my carriage, with sensations which may more easily be conceived than described."

Oct. 31st, 1852.   RODEN.

THE FOLLOWING IS THE ACCOUNT OF HIS VISIT TO FRANCESCO.

"Having arrived here (Volterra) last night, I proceeded at ten o'clock this morning to the great prison, allocated to persons convicted of the worst crimes, containing within its walls at the present time above 500 criminals. . . . On my arrival I was received by the direttore. He introduced me to the sub-direttore, desiring him to conduct me to Madiai's room. We passed through a very long corridor, with cells on either side, and reached the door of the infirmary where Francesco was confined. I was shown into a small room, where the window was on a level with the table, and there was air and light in abundance. Francesco rose from his chair when the sub-direttore told him who I was; he then shut the door and retired, so that I had full opportunity to converse with the prisoner alone. In about a quarter of an hour the sub-direttore returned with the doctor. I thanked them both for their kindness to Francesco, particularly the latter; and I told Madiai, in their hearing, that I was at the head of a deputation which had come from England, France, Germany, Switzerland and Holland, to implore the Grand Duke's clemency towards him and his wife; that, in so doing, we were not only influenced by compassion for them, and the deepest sympathy for their sufferings, but that our special object was to endorse the principle which they had maintained, and for which they were now suffering, namely, that every individual in the world had a right to read the Word of God without note or comment; and that that principle was near and dear to our hearts as Christians. . . . .

"The sub-direttore and doctor having retired, he spoke much to me of the state of his health, saying he was better; but in his weak and reduced frame I could too plainly see the effects of all through which he had passed, and, although comparatively better, I have no doubt that a much longer confinement must terminate in his death. He talked of the comfort which he had in the Scriptures; he found the testimony of the Lord Jesus in them his great support; he cared little for other books in comparison with the Word of God; he was allowed the Roman Catholic Bible by Martini, with notes. . . .

"I found in Francesco Madiai a simple-minded Christian, greatly depressed and worn down by severe suffering, mental and bodily. He made no complaints, and spoke with the greatest respect of the Grand Duke his sovereign, to whom, I had previously heard, he had been always a most attached and loyal subject. He evidently would have entered more at length into the particulars of his case, but I told him that I already knew them. When I asked him if I could do anything for him, he said, " Nothing but to pray for him." I then offered up a short prayer with him for the continuance of God's favour and support towards him and his wife, and bade him farewell with feelings kindred to those with which I had taken leave of his poor wife."

RODEN.

The information received from Florence since the return of the deputation, has been of a conflicting character. According to some accounts the Madiai are soon to be released: according to others, they are to be dealt with more rigorously, and every means employed to induce them to apostatize. It was at one time hoped that at the *accouchement* of his duchess, the Grand Duke would liberate them, but this expectation has not been realized. On the other hand, the spirit of persecution seems to have gathered increased audacity and recklessness. A correspondent of the "Daily News" writing from Florence, on Nov. 13th, says, "The Grand Duke braves it out. He affects to despise the execration of Europe, and causes it to be understood, that the imprisonment of the Madiai is but a slight foretaste of the zeal which he is prepared to exhibit as a true son of the church. He has been heard to say 'I will root out heresy from my dominions, though I should be regarded as the bloodiest tyrant known to history.'" How well does this agree with what is stated in the "Morning Chronicle" for Nov. 25th. "The Grand Duke of Tuscany has issued a decree dated Florence, 16th inst., which, after reciting in the preamble that crimes against public and private security have increased to an alarming extent, and that it has consequently been found necessary to increase the severity of the laws, *re-establishes the punishment of death by the guillotine, for crimes* of public violence against the government, and *against religion*, of high treason, of premeditated homicide and robbery, accompanied by violence. Sentence of death may be pronounced even when the judges are not unanimous on the point."

It will be seen from these communications that should anything be wrung from the Grand Duke by the expostulations which have been addressed to him, nothing can be hoped for from his clemency. He seems determined to act the persecutor. He had stated, it seems, that he cannot "*conscientiously*" act otherwise than he has acted! But the Jesuits are the keepers of his conscience. He seems to have delivered himself up to them, bound hand and foot, and to be acting under their instigation. Our worst wish for him is that he may be dealt with as another noted persecutor of former days was dealt with, who says regarding himself, " I verily thought with myself, that I ought to do many things contrary to the name of Jesus of Nazareth. Which thing I also did in Jerusalem: and many of the saints did I shut up in prison, having received authority from the chief priests; and when they were put to death, I gave my voice against them." (Acts XXVI, 9-10.) But he could also say, " I obtained mercy." May the Grand Duke of Tuscany obtain mercy: such mercy as Saul of Tarsus obtained, that he may eventually become a helper and diffuser of that truth, which he is now seeking to hinder and destroy.

Such then, are the leading facts connected with this most extraordinary and melancholy persecution: for is it not most extraordinary and melancholy, that such deeds can be perpetrated in the middle of the nineteenth century; in an age which we are accustomed to regard as one of enlightenment, of advancement, and of liberty? In Italy, they seem to be going back again to the dark ages! And no doubt the priests of that country would like to bring back those days when the Bible was unprinted, un-translated into the vernaculars; when there was no *Protestant* England to trouble them; when the authority of the Pope and the Popish hierarchy, was undisputed; and when the population of Europe, bound with the chains of ignorance and superstition, lay helpless, submissive, crouching at their feet! These were the palmy days of Popery. But thank God, we live in the nineteenth century and not in the thirteenth, and all the efforts of the Romish Church to roll back the wheels of time will prove unavailing.

But is not the Romish Church throughout Europe responsible for these persecutions? Is not the Pope and the Italian priesthood responsible for them? And Cardinal Wiseman, and the Romish Bishops and Priests in Great Britain and Ireland—are not they responsible for them? It is well known that Rome is *bound* to persecute by the decrees of her own infallible councils. She has never repealed those decrees, and *cannot* repeal them without relinquishing her claim to infallibility, by admitting that she has done wrong in enacting them. The

Romish Church is essentially a persecuting church. What she is doing at Florence is just a specimen of what she would regard it as her duty to do, *if she had the power,* over the whole world. It is what she would do in our own country, *if she could.* No doubt she thinks that what is good for Florentines, would be equally good for Englishmen. The only reason why she does not administer similar discipline to *us,* is, because *she cannot.* Let her once possess the power, and she will not be slow to exercise it.

There are many in these days who appear to think that Popery has become entirely changed; that it is quite a different thing now, from what it was some centuries ago; that from being a blood-thirsty tiger, it has become a gentle, harmless lamb, that may be caressed and fondled without danger. It may be hoped that these notorious facts, which have drawn on them so much of the public notice, are somewhat opening men's eyes, and convincing them that Popery is unchanged and unchangeable; that it is essentially the same everywhere— the same in England, as in Florence, and at Rome.

We have said that Cardinal Wiseman and the Romish priesthood in this country are responsible for these persecutions. They are members of the church by whose authority, and at whose bidding this thing is done. They have sworn allegiance to that church. And they lift no protest against these persecutions. Not a solitary individual among them, so far as we can ascertain, has come forward publicly to disavow and denounce them. If it was a right thing that a deputation should go to Florence to remonstrate against the iniquitous sentence passed on the Madiai, it would have been right that the members of it had been Romish Ecclesiastics. Cardinal Wiseman ought to have been at the head of it. Some of the most noted among the priestly agitators for "religious equality" should have supported it. Had they disapproved of the persecution, they ought to have been ready to have renounced their connection with the church in which they minister, unless the Pope had himself sanctioned their deputation, and given it his support. But instead of thus bestirring themselves with indignant zeal to wipe out the stigma with which this persecution brands them, they *do* nothing; they *say* nothing; they keep perfectly quiet about it. Are they not then sanctioning it by their silence? But if Mr. Lucas may be regarded as the exponent of their sentiments, they approve of it, and are prepared to defend it! This distinguished ornament of their church, the editor of their leading newspaper, and member of Parliament for Meath, who unblushingly avows that "he has burnt a Protestant Bible, and is prepared to burn a thousand more," says, in defending this persecution, "In the former case" (when a country is exclusively popish) "no native inhabitant of the state can become a Protestant without committing a crime against God, and without inflicting an injury upon society. If I were the ruler of such a state I would not allow the foreign preacher to sow his noxious seed among the good corn: and in the kind of repression to be used for preventing the first introduction of heresy, I would be guided by the circumstances of the case, and by considerations of expediency." Happily, Mr. Lucas' supposition is not likely to be realized. He will never become the ruler of such a state! There can be no doubt however that in such a case, he would do with Protestants as he now thinks it expedient to do with their Bibles. He would consume both in the same fires! Let us learn then, the tender mercies we may expect to experience from the Romish church, should she ever acquire in our country the power she is seeking. The fires of persecution would be kindled up in England to-morrow if Rome could kindle them; just as, were it not for Protestant power and influence, they would be blazing at the present time throughout Italy!

The Roman Catholic laity need not be included in this condemnation. We believe that many of them are better than their creed. It gives us pleasure to quote on this point the following testimony from a recent letter of Sir Culling Eardley to Lord Shaftesbury. "It is within my knowledge, both from conversation and respondence, that the indignation felt by Roman Catholics is almost equal to that of Protestants. . . . Let us not in this matter confound the Roman Catholic laity in general with the priests and their subservient instruments." No one can have read the denunciation of the conduct of the Duke of Tuscany by Mr. Sergeant Shee, and one or two others of the Romish laity, without satisfaction. Let Rome but persevere in the course she is now pursuing, and she will soon succeed in effectually alienating from herself the confidence and affections of the best among those who now glory in their connection with her.

But this leads us to the further observation that *these Florentine persecutions are defeating their own end.* The object of the Grand Duke in thus " breathing out threatenings and slaughter," and of the Jesuits who are hounding him on, is to prevent the spread of Bible truth, and to exterminate heresy. It is for this purpose that the police are now " entering every house," where the gospel is confessed, and "haling men and women, are committing them to prison." It is for this purpose that hundreds are now pining in the prisons of Tuscany, and that decapitation by the guillotine is threatened. But how does the work of these modern persecutors prosper? Just as did that of their prototypes in Jerusalem, when the Gospel was first proclaimed. The Scriptures are circulated and read in spite of all opposition. Numbers are being awakened to enquiry and reflection. The desire to become acquainted with that truth for which so many are suffering is spreading like a contagion. Sympathy with the sufferers for conscience sake, even among Romanists, is almost universal. The correspondent of the " Daily News" writing from Florence in Nov. last, says, " Protestantism is here rapidly increasing, and the Jesuits are every day more and more alarmed at the growing spirit of revolt" (from Popery.) In another more recent communication he says, " we remain in expectation of further and more rigorous measures to put a stop to the Protestant movement. The government is aware that the presence of the deputation has inspired the Protestants here with renewed confidence in the ultimate triumph of their principles, and that an address expressive of this sentiment, emanating from a very numerous body, and thanking their Christian friends of different states for their exertions in favour of the Madiai, was placed in the hands of Lord Roden before his departure."

Such is the result of persecution in the nineteenth century. It is like throwing oil upon fire, causing it to burn brighter, and spread more extensively. We have been informed that wherever the members of the deputation were recognised in Piedmont, Tuscany, &c., they were received with acclamations, and that the authorities were unable to prevent the manifestation of popular enthusiasm. At the railway stations, on the public streets, at the prison gates, wherever they showed themselves, they were welcomed with most cordial expressions of good-will. There was no manifestation of feeling of the opposite kind. The sympathies of almost the entire community appeared to be on the side of the persecuted. It cannot now be doubted that the population in the North of Italy is very extensively alienated from Romanism; and that were the people but free to follow their convictions, there would soon be less Popery in those parts of Italy than their is in England. It would disappear like a stone cast into the sea, and be found no more.

We seem now to be getting into the very heat of the last great conflict with Popery. Her emissaries are everywhere busy—busier now, perhaps, than ever before. With them it is a death struggle. It is a struggle for life, and for what is dearer to them than life—for empire and prolonged dominion. It is for this purpose that Popery is now allying herself with the despotic powers on the continent. It is for this purpose that she is supporting Louis Napoleon, and lauding the author of the Parisian massacre as a saint, and almost as a demi-god. It is for this purpose that she has recently instigated the Emperor of Austria to banish the Bible from his dominions. It is for this pupose that she sustains the King of Naples in detaining trom 15,000 to 20.000 Neapolitans in prison for slight political offences. It is for this purpose that the Pontifical government, after detaining numbers of her subjects in confinement for 3½ years, for the same cause, many of them husbands and fathers, is now leading them forth in bands, day after day, to be shot. And it is for this purpose she is now seeking extended political power in England.

But it cannot succeed. Popery is doomed, and the time of her destruction is fast coming on. God in his Providence is permitting her at the present time to perpetrate these barbarous atrocities, that her *real character* may be displayed before the world, and that men may thus be prepared to join in the song of exultation over her downfall. That downfall is at hand. Already we see the signs of its approach. It is evident that if Popery is *outwardly strengthening* by allying herself with despotism, she is *inwardly weakening* by losing the sympathies of the people. The people of Tuscany and Sardinia, in masses, are hastening out of Rome. The same change is rapidly going forward among the Irish, and to some extent, also, in France, in Belgium, and in other parts of Europe.

Popery is thus, at present, losing far more ground than she is gaining. She numbers those who enter her communion by *units*, but she has to number those who are leaving it by *thousands*. Is not this the response of those she has so long deceived to the invitation, " Come out of her, my people, that ye be not partakers of her sins, and that ye receive not of her plagues ?" Rev. xviii, 4. Her destruction is foretold as coming suddenly, when she is in the very height of prosperity, and it will be terrible, overwhelming, complete. " She saith in her heart, I sit a queen, and am no widow, and shall see no sorrow. Therefore shall her plagues come in one day, death, and mourning, and famine ; and she shall be utterly burned with fire : for strong is the Lord God who judgeth her." Rev. xviii. 7-8.

Such is the long predicted, and now approaching doom of this great enemy of the cause of God. Let British Christians beware how they tamper with her, or give her any kind of aid or encouragement. Let them learn to regard her in her true character as portrayed in the Word of God, and written in letters of blood, in her own past history. Popery is not Christianity, but the great apostacy from Christianity. It is not Christ, but Antichrist. It is not so much a religion, as a great organized conspiracy against the liberties and happiness of mankind.

The church of Christ moreover has no cause to fear as to the issue of the great conflict in which she is now called to engage. It may be severe, but it will be brief. It will issue in the destruction not only of Popery, but also of every system that bears in any measure its image and superscription. Scriptural Christianity is the only true Christianity. Nothing else will stand the test of the trying day that is at hand. The language of the Apostle (HEB. XII. 26-29) will prove in the issue to be strictly applicable to the times that are fast coming on us. "Yet once more I shake not the earth only, but also heaven"—not the world only, but also the church—things ecclesiastical, as well as things civil. "And this word, Yet once more, signifieth the removing of those things that are shaken, as of things that are made, that those things which cannot be shaken may remain." And surely such things as apostolical succession, baptismal regeneration, and *priestism* in every form, are not among the things which cannot be shaken, and are therefore to remain; but among those which will be found wanting in the day of trial, and will therefore be swept away, and be found no more. Let Christians then, the subjects of the "kingdom which cannot be moved, have grace, whereby they may serve God acceptably with reverence and godly fear." "Their God is a consuming fire." Let them be jealous, then, for his honour. Let them cleave to his truth, as set forth in his word, discarding the "doctrines and commandments of men." Then when He comes as a consuming fire, there will be the less in them for the consuming fire to destroy. Then they will enter the immovable kingdom—immovable because founded on truth, and therefore enduring for ever.

STIDOLPH AND SONS, PRINTERS, TUNBRIDGE WELLS.

www.ingramcontent.com/pod-product-compliance
Lightning Source LLC
Chambersburg PA
CBHW081307040426
42452CB00014B/2690